Red Planet Rescue

Red Planet Rescue

Lindsay Galvin

Illustrated by Alan Brown

Collins

Contents

Chapter 1	2
Chapter 2	12
Chapter 3	20
Chapter 4	30
Chapter 5	39
Chapter 6	49
Teaching Mum!	58
Maglev really exists!	60
Mars fact file	62
Could people really live on Mars?	64
How would people breathe and grow food?	66
Green Mars on Red Alert!	68
About the author	70
About the illustrator	72
Book chat	74

Chapter 1

Bo's mum is a scientist working on the planet Mars for a company called Green Mars Inc. She grows plants in domes.

How was school?

OK, I suppose.

All the scientists' families live together in a big apartment block. This means they can all take turns looking after the kids, who all go to the same school.

How is Mars today?

More windy than usual. There might be another storm.

If Mum's experiments are successful, one day crops will grow on Mars, so people can live there.

Why are Clicker's eyes so bright? They aren't getting hot again, are they?

Maybe a bit.

Clicker used to be a computer mouse in the old days. Bo's mum made him into a robot.

You can fix his eyes yourself, Bo.

I don't want to break him. I'll wait for you to get home.

Click!

Bo and her friends have a routine – every night after school they ride their maglev boards. These are like skateboards from the old days, but work using magnets.

Sometimes Mum's calls cut out. After all, Mars is 228 million kilometres away!

If you're riding tonight, why not try the half-pipe? It's fun to have new experiences, Bo. Now, wear your helmet and check ...

4

The old factory used to make sweets. But now treats come out of special machines instead, and the old factory is a maglev skate park.

Hey!

Hey!

Hey!

Darian's here. He's such a bully! Why doesn't he like you, Bo?

Let's just stay out of his way, guys.

Because she's his little sister, and she's got better technique!

The speediest place to ride is on the steel stair railings way up high. The edges of the big metal storage containers are a fun place to get your riding technique just right.

Come on, Darian's on the storage containers, so let's ride the rails.

OK. Quickly, while he's not looking.

Bo and her friends check their safety cords and then check each other's too. They wear magnetic boots, but the cord is important in case they fall off their maglev boards.

Bo gathers speed on the rails, even though she's going uphill. She tries some daring tricks.

Pop!

Grind!

Spin!

At the top, Clicker seems upset. Bo thinks maybe he's broken ... or maybe he knows something she doesn't. All Bo can see are the rails and the kids cheering down below.

Quiet, Clicker! Stay in my pocket. This is going to get fast. Cord – check. Helmet – check.

Click clickedy click.

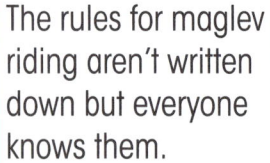

The rules for maglev riding aren't written down but everyone knows them.

1. Never touch another rider's kit.
2. Check your cord.
3. Take turns.

Move, little squirts.

But there's someone coming down.

She'll only be a second. Bo is so fast.

You think Bo is fast?

Oh yes, Darian, you know she's the fastest here, her technique is amazing —

Shhh!

Why don't we find out how good my little sis really is?

The maglev boards stay on the rails whatever happens, as long as there is the right kind of metal. But the kids riding them ... well, let's just say that's why you always check your cord.

What is he doing? I can't stop! Can't he see me?

Out of the way!

We'll see who is fastest now.

Click click click.

Bo hasn't tried this trick before.
Mum would say it was a bit precarious ...

Everyone down below is staring as Bo swings through the air on her cord. She does a spin, then a somersault.

Clicker!

Am I going to make it?

Go, Bo! Look at those tricks.

Not that stupid mouse robot?

Give him back!

I could easily crush it. Hey, make it stop stinging me!

Bo's wrist screen vibrates. It's Win's mum, Tisha, calling. Bo and Darian are staying with Win and Tisha while Mum is on Mars.

Hi, Bo and Win, there's a huge windstorm on Mars. The power lines have been damaged.

Is Mum safe?

Mum and the scientists are fine, they have back-up powerpacks for their habitat dome.

What about the plant domes?

The power will last until tomorrow. Hopefully we'll find a way to get some powerpacks out to them.

Chapter 2

Later, Tisha tells Bo and Darian how the storm on Mars has cut off the electricity where Mum works. All the Green Mars Inc plant domes are out of power. The plants can't survive without heat and light.

Can't they just get back-up powerpacks for the plant domes?

The vehicles won't work in this storm. They can't get to them.

But they have to save Mum's plants!

Bo can't sleep. She keeps thinking about when she last visited Mum on Mars. Mum showed her an old shaft near the domes that led to a tunnel.

Don't go in too far, Bo.

Where do these tunnels go?

They lead back to the wormhole we use to travel here from Earth.

Bo had kicked aside the dust and had seen the thick cables.

So we could walk to the wormhole from here?

No – part of the tunnel has vertical drops.

I could ride my maglev board. You know I can zoom up the tunnel wall!

Oh, Bo! It's possible ... but I think it would be too precarious.

Now Bo kicks off her bedcovers. She could take a powerpack through those tunnels on her maglev board.

Click.

Shhhhh!

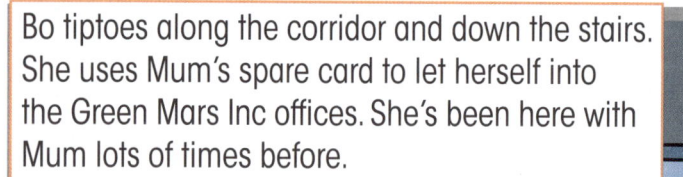

Bo tiptoes along the corridor and down the stairs. She uses Mum's spare card to let herself into the Green Mars Inc offices. She's been here with Mum lots of times before.

Come on, Clicker, let's go to Mum's office and find that map of the tunnels.

Click.

Shhh!

There is already a person sitting at Mum's screen, and it looks like a kid … He spins around.

Darian!

Bo!

What are you doing here?

When he sees Bo, Darian tries to cover the screen.

You found the tunnel map!

I wanted to find out if there was any more news. I care about Mum too.

What do you know about the tunnels?

Show me what you are hiding, Darian. Go on, Clicker.

Bo ignores Darian's question, she doesn't trust him. She clicks her wrist screen, taking a photo of the map.

Bo heads towards the kit room. Darian follows her.
Hey – where are you going?
Me and my brother working together is not a thing!
I'm going this way too, actually.
I'm doing something important here. Please go away.
I'm on a mission. This needs a hero.
What mission?
I'm going to ride through the old cable tunnels to take a powerpack to the domes.
That's my idea!

Bo and Darian get in each other's way as they grab Mars suits.

I'm doing this mission, Darian.

You're too slow. The plants will be dead by the time you get there.

Bo and Darian stand glaring at each other. Neither wants to be the first one to look away.

Click click click.

You're right, Clicker. Mum and her plants need us. Fine, Darian. If we both go, at least we can carry two power packs.

That was exactly what I was going to say.

visor – helps you breathe

suit – for warmth

torch

heavy magnetic boots

17

Mars has less gravity than Earth. Make sure you put your boots on properly so you don't float off.

Bo and Darian agree on one thing — they need to look at the map to work out the way. There is only one safe path through the tunnels.

Look, there are hazards. We need to avoid those.

Click click.

What did it say?

We need to work together.

Bo and Darian collect the powerpacks.

It's so heavy!

It's light as a feather.

They travel down in the lift to the wormhole entrance in the basement. Mum's card lets them in.

Are you ready? Visors down.

Bo ... have you ever travelled by wormhole on your own before?

Of course not. We always go in pairs.

I mean without Mum.

Clicker thinks you are nervous, Darian.

Clicker can shhh!

Here.

Chapter 3

Bo, Darian and Clicker tumble inside the wormhole, spinning through time and space. In what feels like seconds they have travelled 228 million kilometres.

Mum does this all the time. She says it's quite relaxing once you get used to it.

Click clickedy click!

Help!

They are hurtling towards the red planet, Mars, and their mission to save the plants is about to begin.

Let go!

I was just checking you weren't too scared. Now – Mission Mars!

But you were holding on to me so tight, you almost crushed my hand!

Hey, you've landed on Clicker. Move! You've broken him.

Whoops. There, he's OK. He's fine now, look.

Click clickedy CLICK!

Owwww! Stop trying to hurt me, mouse!

Well, you did sit on him!

You're all right now, Clicker.

Keep that junk away from me, Bo, I mean it.

Bo, Darian and Clicker head out of the wormhole onto Mars. The storm rages, with wind and dust sweeping around them. Luckily, they are right next to the tunnel entrance.

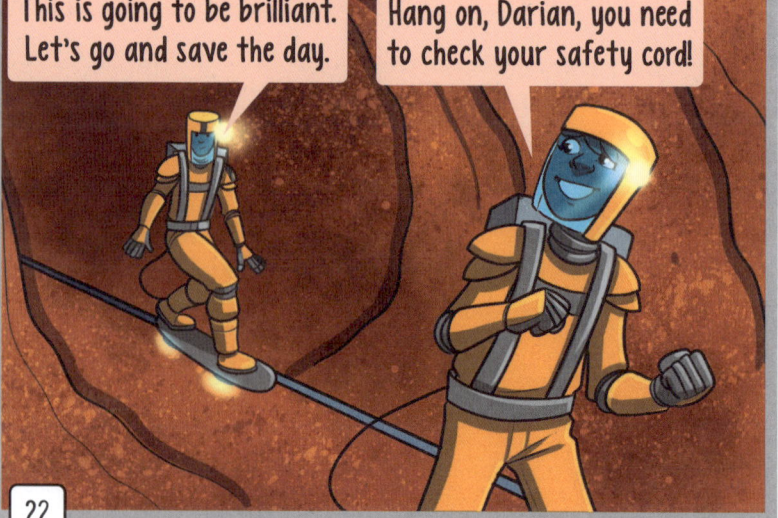

"Phew, this is the tunnel."

"Look, under this dust, these are the old cables."

"This is going to be brilliant. Let's go and save the day."

"Hang on, Darian, you need to check your safety cord!"

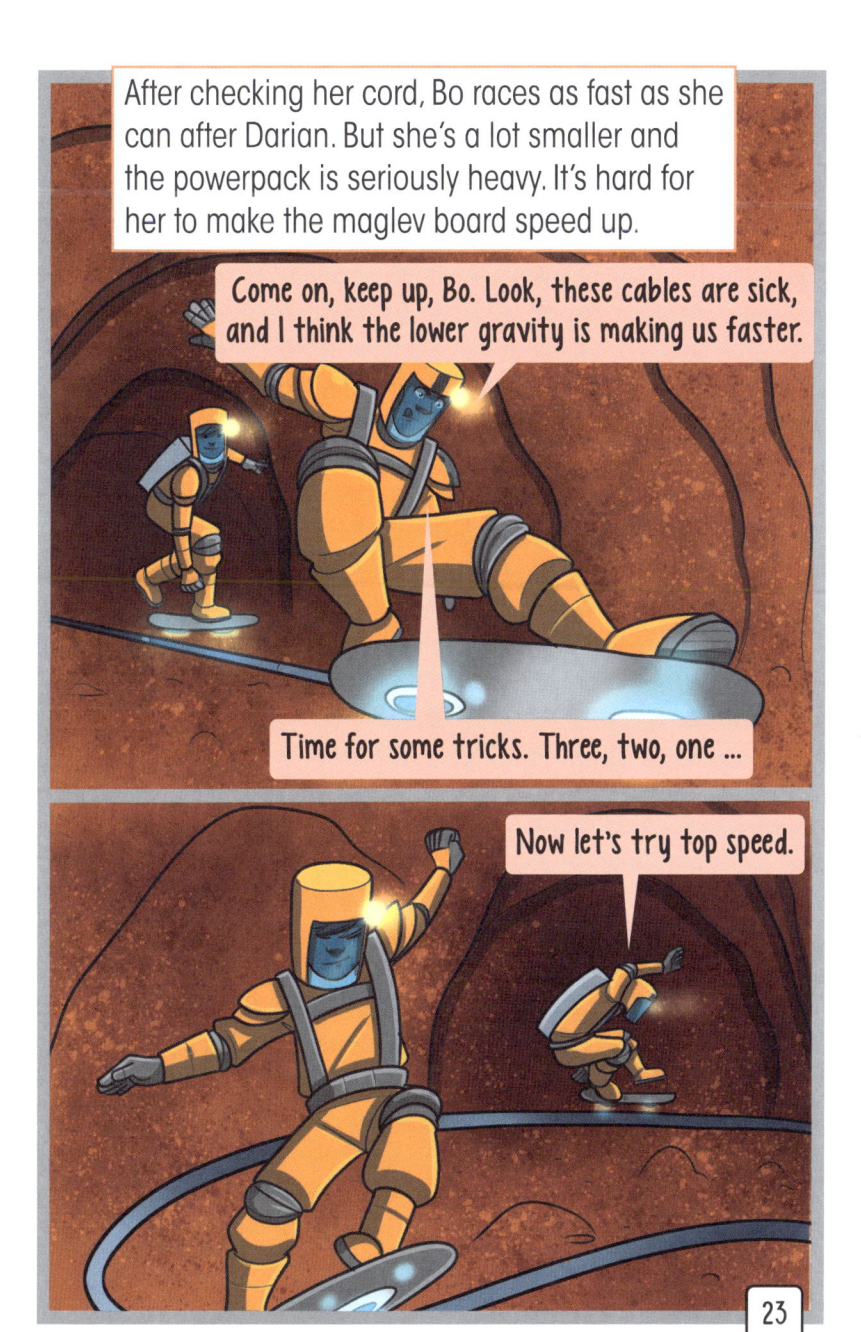

After checking her cord, Bo races as fast as she can after Darian. But she's a lot smaller and the powerpack is seriously heavy. It's hard for her to make the maglev board speed up.

Come on, keep up, Bo. Look, these cables are sick, and I think the lower gravity is making us faster.

Time for some tricks. Three, two, one ...

Now let's try top speed.

Bo is left behind in the dark tunnel. It's scary, but she knows there's no way she can catch up with Darian.

Looks like I'm on my own.

Clickedy click.

Sorry, Clicker, of course you're here too. We'll be OK. Let's go and find Mum.

Thump!

What was that? Where is this dust coming from?

Click CLICK!

Don't be scared, Clicker, it must be Darian.

There's no such thing as Mars monsters, silly.

Bo zooms off into the dusty darkness ahead, and almost crashes into Darian coming in the other direction.

There you are!

Why isn't your head torch on? You almost crashed straight into us. What happened?

The tunnel goes straight up, just up ahead. I smashed into the wall and broke my head torch.

Did you hurt yourself?

No way, I'm made of strong stuff. But I think I'll wear my cord now.

I did remind you!

The tunnel feels much scarier now they only have one head torch. Soon they have to ride straight upwards. Bo is glad when the tunnel straightens out again.

"Why have you stopped?"

"I have an idea. Give me your head torch. I'll go ahead and come back for you."

"No! We should stay together. Last time you went ahead, you crashed!"

Give me the torch, Bo.

No, Darian, you aren't having my torch! You'll ruin the mission.

Bo is furious and races off, leaving Darian behind in the dark tunnel with no torch.

Click click click.

It's his own fault, Clicker. He shouldn't have smashed his torch and then tried to steal mine.

Click click.

I'm not going back for him, I've tried being in a team.

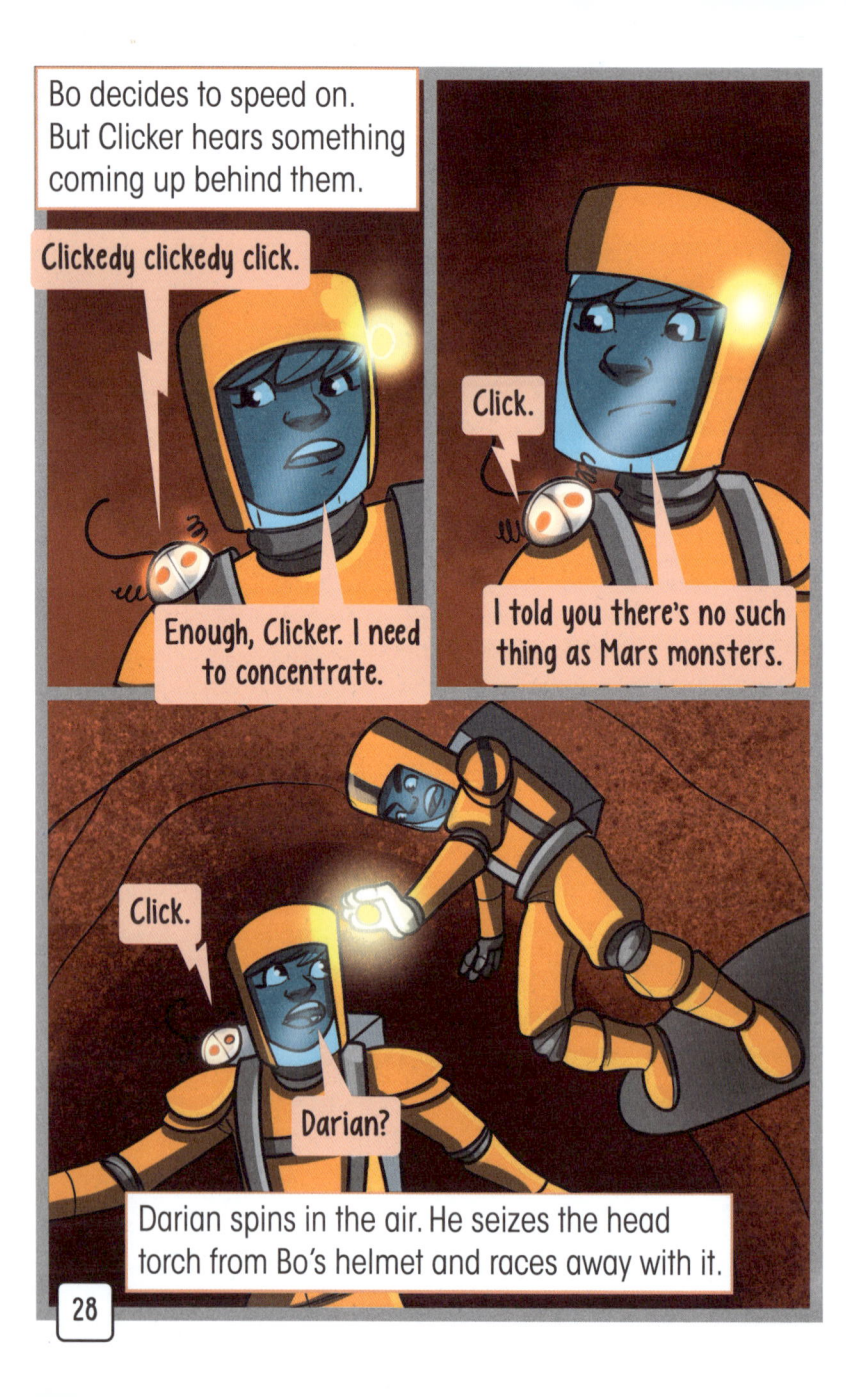

Bo decides to speed on. But Clicker hears something coming up behind them.

Clickedy clickedy click.

Enough, Clicker. I need to concentrate.

Click.

I told you there's no such thing as Mars monsters.

Click.

Darian?

Darian spins in the air. He seizes the head torch from Bo's helmet and races away with it.

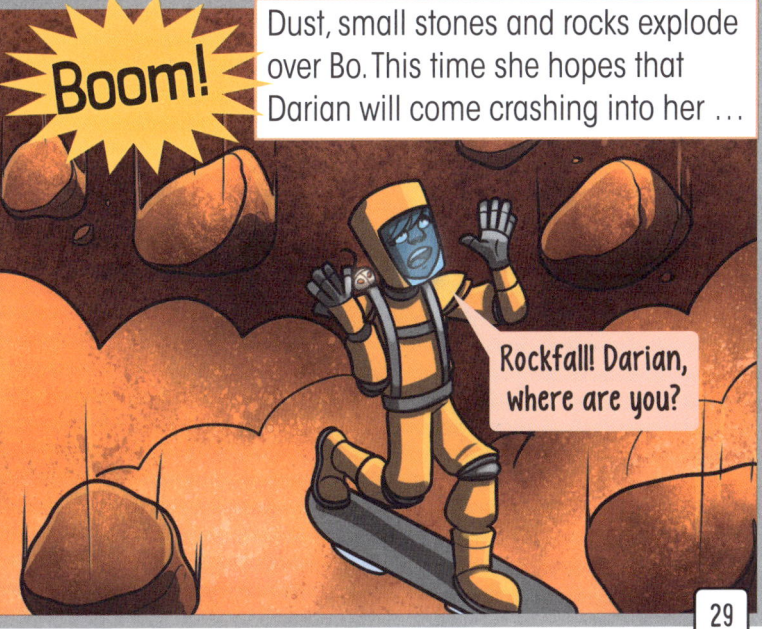

Bo is left in the dark as Darian races off again. It is pitch black in the tunnel.

Clicker, are you there?

Your glowing eyes! Thank goodness I didn't fix them.

Rumble

Did you hear that? The whole tunnel is shaking. Come on, we need to find Darian.

Boom!

Dust, small stones and rocks explode over Bo. This time she hopes that Darian will come crashing into her …

Rockfall! Darian, where are you?

CHAPTER 4

When the small stones and dust have stopped raining down on her from the tunnel ceiling, Bo stands up. Her visor is opaque with dust and she wipes it clean.

Darian! Darian, can you hear me? Maybe Darian was ahead of the rockfall. Let's move some rocks.

Bo wishes they hadn't tried this mission. Now Darian might be under the rocks, injured. She starts to heave the heavy rocks but some are too big to lift.

Darian! Darian! It's no good, Clicker. I can't do any more.

Clickedy click.

Yes! I can use the maglev board as a shovel. It's OK, Darian, we're coming!

Bo stands at the back of her maglev board, and uses her feet to guide it. Once she's got the hang of it, it works as an excellent shovel.

Bo? Hello, can you hear me?

Darian! Is that you? I'm coming! Are you hurt?

No – I'm in a kind of cave.

Listen, Darian. I'll tell you how to dig yourself out.

Bo moves some more of the rocks so Darian can hear what she is saying.

Bo, are you still there?

Yes, I'm right here. Now use your board to help you dig.

OK, I'm trying. It's small in here. Bo – don't leave me, will you?

Of course I won't.

Click clickedy click.

Good idea, Clicker.

Clicker can come through the little gaps to keep you company if you like.

Yes please.

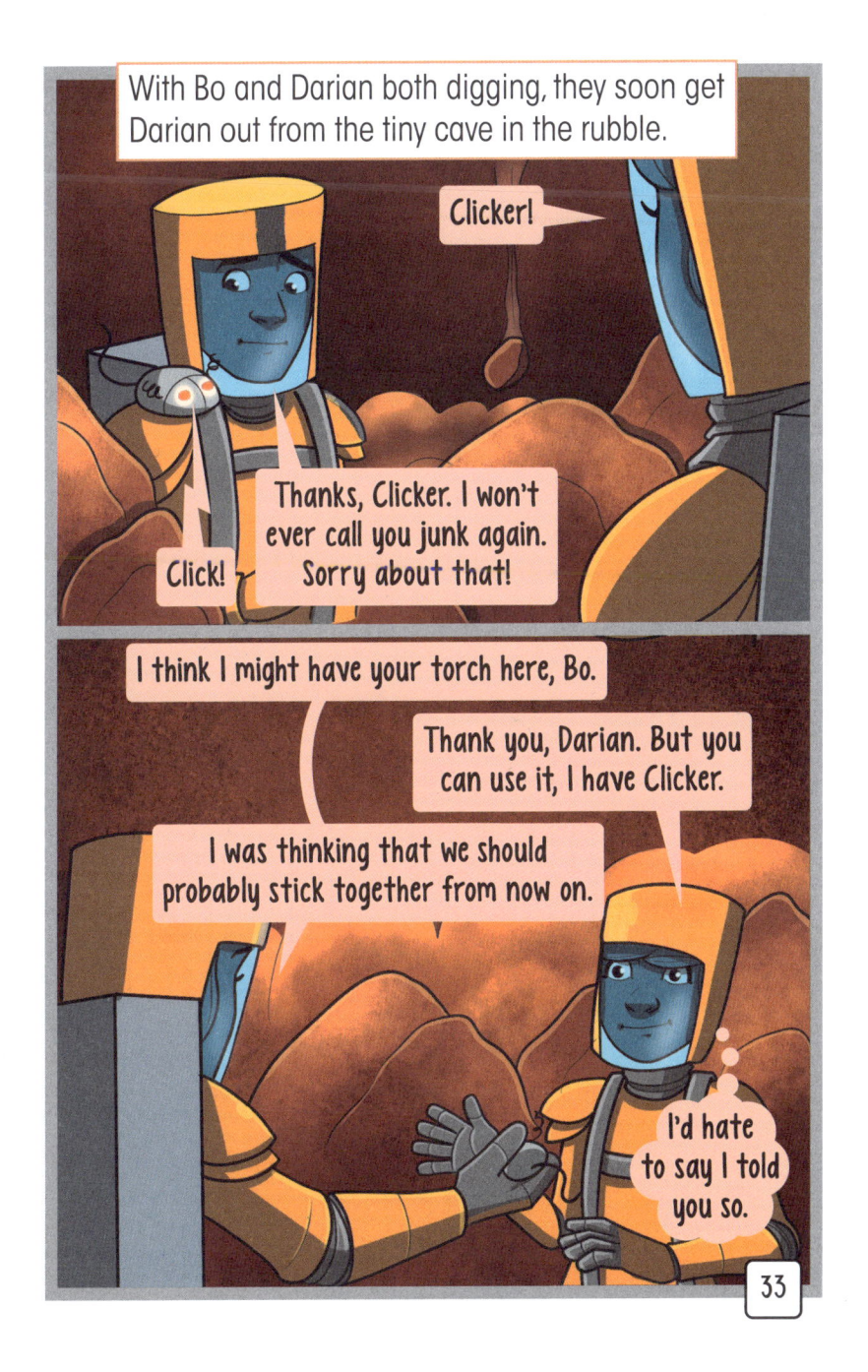

With Bo and Darian both digging, they soon get Darian out from the tiny cave in the rubble.

Clicker!

Click!

Thanks, Clicker. I won't ever call you junk again. Sorry about that!

I think I might have your torch here, Bo.

Thank you, Darian. But you can use it, I have Clicker.

I was thinking that we should probably stick together from now on.

I'd hate to say I told you so.

When they try to clear a way through the rest of the rockfall, they realise the tunnel is blocked. They will have to go back and take another way.

"Let's see if there's a way through."

"Every way has hazards."

They ride back down the tunnel and take a new turning.

"You can lead with Clicker, if you like. His eyes are brighter than the torch."

"It's OK to admit you are scared."

"Scared? Me?"

"STOP!"

"The cables are broken!"

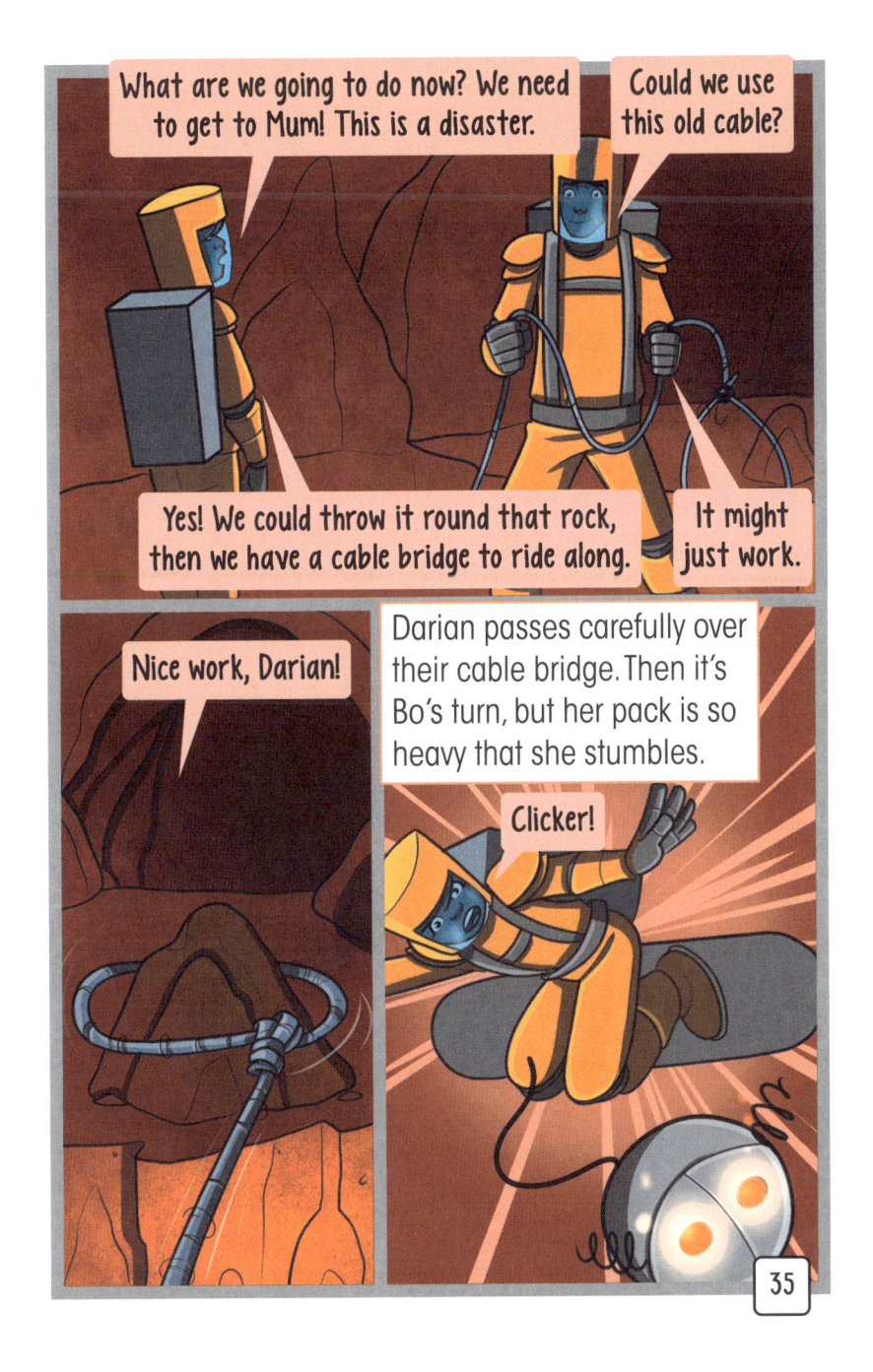

"What are we going to do now? We need to get to Mum! This is a disaster."

"Could we use this old cable?"

"Yes! We could throw it round that rock, then we have a cable bridge to ride along."

"It might just work."

"Nice work, Darian!"

Darian passes carefully over their cable bridge. Then it's Bo's turn, but her pack is so heavy that she stumbles.

"Clicker!"

Clicker! Are you OK? Clicker!

Clickedy click.

I can't leave him. I've got to go down there.

You can't do that!

I have to. So think, Darian, we have to make a plan. You are good at plans.

Am I good at plans?

I know – what about that scary trick you did in the factory, when you swung on your cord?

Great idea. I can climb down my suit's safety cord!

Darian waits in the tunnel, with the other end of the suit's safety cord knotted tightly around a rock. Bo climbs down.

Is the cord strong enough?

It's a safety cord, Darian!

Ha ha! I do know that.

She climbs down carefully and picks up Clicker.

Gotcha! Pull us up, Darian.

The cord is caught!

Clickedy click.

Are you sure?

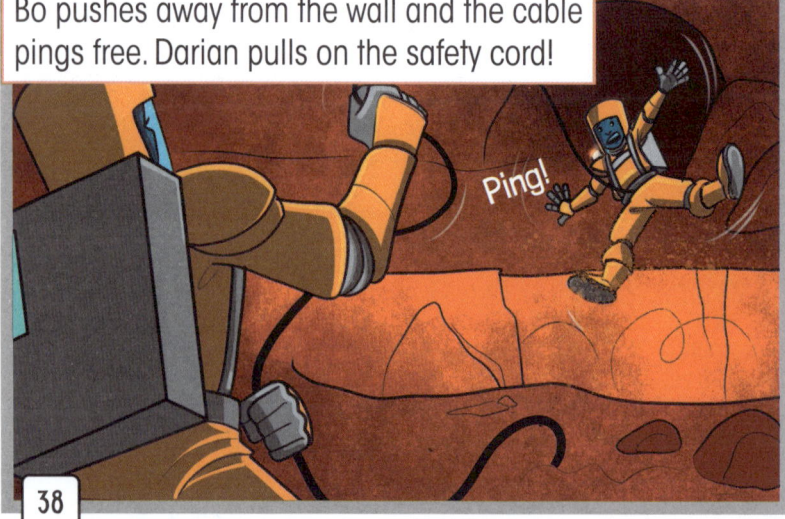

"I know, I'll push away from the wall to free the cord and you pull hard."

"You'll be too heavy for me to pull up!"

"Remember we are lighter on Mars. Ready?"

"Ready."

Bo pushes away from the wall and the cable pings free. Darian pulls on the safety cord!

Ping!

Chapter 5

Bo, Darian and Clicker are a team again. But when they ride around the next corner they meet another problem.

Ouch! How am I going to ride in this wind tunnel?

Ooof! Try again, I'll be right behind you ...

Shall we go back again?

I don't think there's another way and this wind is too strong for me with the pack.

CRASH!

You should go on alone.

"I can't leave you here, Bo. I'm sorry that I left you before."

"I don't think we have much choice now!"

"OK I'll go ahead, but I promise I'll come straight back."

"You should take Clicker with you. Just in case there is another rockfall."

"No – Clicker stays with you."

Bo and Clicker wait in the dark tunnel. The wind batters them so they shelter in a dip.

It feels like Darian has been gone hours, although Bo's screen tells her it has only been a few minutes. She starts imagining all sorts of horrible things.

I wish I'd checked his safety cord, Clicker.

Clickedy click.

You saw him put it on? That's good. What if he gets lost?

Bo is so busy thinking, that she's startled when Darian is suddenly there.

There you are! Are you all right?

Just tired. That was hard. The wind is coming from a hole in the ceiling. It's OK on the other side.

I'll take your pack.

Where is your pack? Have you lost it?

I left it the other side of the hole, so I can carry yours.

Bo understands Darian's idea. It will be so much easier for her to ride without her pack in this wind. But Darian is tired out.

"Here, let me check the straps and your safety cord."

"I'm going to check yours too, Bo!"

"That's not like you, Darian."

"It is now! No more disasters. We need to get to the domes."

"So you can be a hero?"

"Of course! But only because you are a hero too."

Now Bo has an idea. If Bo leads the way and Darian rides close behind, he'll be sheltered from the wind.

Follow me.

They speed up, with the Mars storm wind whistling past them, until they pass the hole in the ceiling.

There's your powerpack.

The map says the way should be clear now.

They race towards the end of the tunnel.

We're here!

What if we are too late?

At first Bo and Darian think the Green Mars Inc domes are in complete darkness. But as they get closer, they see the sleeping dome is dimly lit.

"Mum!"

"Bo, Darian! What on earth are you doing here?"

"We've got you some presents!"

"Powerpacks? Just in time, the power in the domes only went off a few minutes ago."

"Mars Riders to the rescue!"

"But how did you get these here?"

"We rode our maglev boards through the old cable tunnels."

The scientists connect the powerpacks to the Green Mars Inc domes.

"I admit that I'm a bit surprised to see you two here together."

"We worked as a team, Mum."

"Well, you did a brilliant job. Well done, both of you!"

Everyone cheers when the lights and heating come back on. All the plants will survive!

"Are you hungry, kids? I've got a surprise for you."

Mum leads Bo and Darian to one of the plant domes. The storm isn't so bad now and the sun shines red through the dust.

What are these?

Our first crop of Mars strawberries!

Are they supposed to be blue?

That's how they grow on Mars. They have been tested and are edible.

Can I try one?

Of course — they would have died if you hadn't got us the powerpacks in time.

Mmmmmm, delicious!

47

The storm has died down. Mum drives Bo and Darian back to the wormhole in her Mars vehicle.

It's easier to travel over Mars than under it!

Only two people can travel through the wormhole at a time. Mum takes Bo's hand.

I'll come back for you Darian, wait here.

It's OK, Mum. Bo and I can go together. You can follow.

Ready, Darian?

I'm always ready, Bo.

Chapter 6

Bo and Darian are back on Earth. The next day is school as normal. There is an announcement in morning assembly.

"Good morning, children, you'll be pleased to hear the Green Mars Inc domes have got their power back on. The plants are saved!"

"Now settle down."

"It was me and Bo who saved them!"

"As if!"

"No way!"

"Darian! No shouting out in assembly. Put your hand up, please."

"They won't believe us, Darian."

"Sorry, Miss!"

49

Back home, Bo tells Mum that no one believed that she and Darian took the powerpacks to Mars.

"Don't worry. There's going to be a surprise tomorrow."

"What sort of surprise?"

"It won't be a surprise if I tell you ..."

Bo asks Mum to help her in the workshop. She is also planning a surprise!

"Do you want to try using the blowtorch?"

"OK. Pass me the gloves."

After school, Bo meets her friends Win and Hamza outside the old factory maglev skate park.
Oh no, Darian is coming. What shall we do?
It's OK. We get along better now.
Seriously? He almost ran you off the rails last time. He tried to crush Clicker, too.
Click!

"Hey, Bo. Hey, Win and Hamza. Are you going in? Ready to ride?"

"Hey."

"Hey."

Win and Hamza are so surprised to see Darian being friendly, they stand there staring.

"Let's ride! But not here, we've done this too many times."

"Mum was right, sometimes it's fun to have a new experience. Follow me."

"Where are we going?"

"You'll just have to trust me."

Bo takes them to the old train station. Long ago, antique trains ran on steel rails. The station also has a roof made of huge steel arches.

This place is incredible! So many places to ride.

Let's check our safety cords.

Did Darian just say check our safety cords? Seriously?

I'll do yours, Bo, if you do mine.

Clickedy click.

Is your helmet new?

Safety first!

The four kids race up and down the steel arches. Sometimes they turn upside down precariously, but their maglev boards grip tight to the steel. They can race side by side because there is much more space.

"Up to your old tricks again. Here."

Swoop

Spin

Grind

This is epic!

Thanks, Darian.

Soon some of the other kids arrive. There's room for everyone.

Boing!

Shall we explore? The rails are long gone but there are still some metal handrails up a long flight of stairs.

Bo, Win and Hamza speed into the tunnel, their way lit up by Clicker. But where is Darian?

I think I might go back now, guys.

Hey, Darian, wait. I have something for you.

For me? My own Clicker? Where did you get it?

I made it! But you can't call her Clicker, she needs her own name.

Click.

Beep.

I'll call her Beepee!

Clicker and Beepee both light the tunnel with their eyes.

55

When they walk out of the train station, Darian whispers to Bo.

Did you tell Hamza and Win about our mission?

Not yet. They'd never believe we did something that heroic!

We saved the plants, but I guess no one will ever know.

Well, I know, and so do all the scientists.

And you, Clicker. That's enough for me.

Click click.

In assembly the next morning, the teacher shows a clip taken by the video cameras on the Mars domes.

Hey, that looks like you, Bo!

Darian? You were really there?

Mum and some other scientists walk into the hall.

Hello everyone, we'd like you to be the first to try ... Mars strawberries!

Bo and Darian, come up here. They rode their maglev boards to bring us the powerpacks.

They saved the first Mars crop through teamwork.

So that was Mum's surprise!

So we are calling these ... Bo-Darian Strawberries!

Bonus
Teaching Mum!

Bo teaches her mum to ride the rails like she does!

trying new things

Mum getting the "hang" of it

Mum the Mars Rider

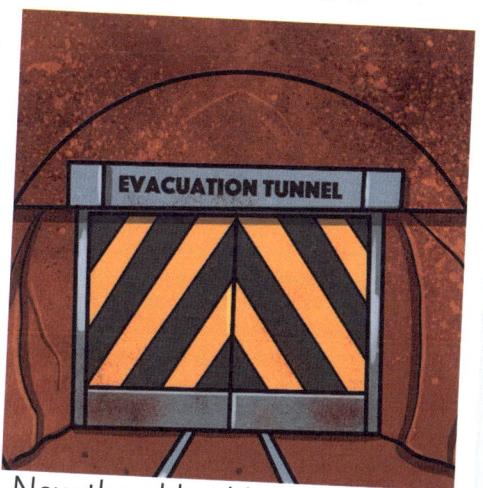

Now the old cable tunnels can be used in emergencies.

Bonus

Maglev really exists!

The magnetic levitation (maglev) technology already exists on rides and trains.

Maglev hover board

This board can lift itself and a rider above the ground.

Magnets and superconductors work together to repel the force of gravity.

The board hovers two and a half centimetres off the ground.

Maglev train

The magnetic plates contain very strong magnets that pass their magnetic field on to the metal surface. That becomes a magnet too! Then when the two magnets repel each other – the train hovers.

Maglev trains need a special surface to travel on.

Mars fact file

- Mars is named after the Roman god of war.
- It is the fourth planet from the sun in the same solar system as Earth.
- It about half the size of Earth.
- It has two moons.

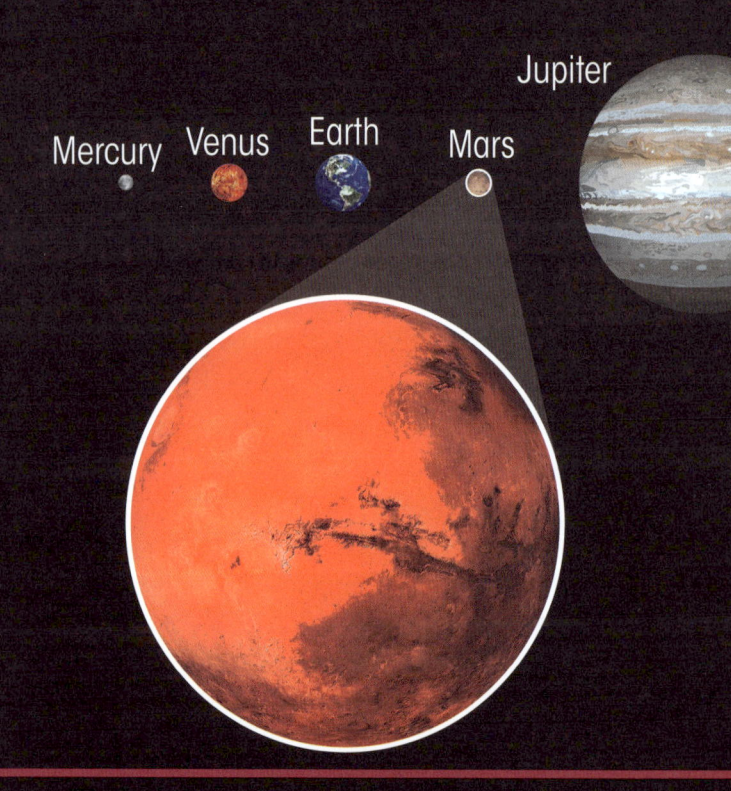

- No humans have been to Mars … yet! But some robots have!

- Some parts of Mars are very cold: minus 140 degrees Celsius.

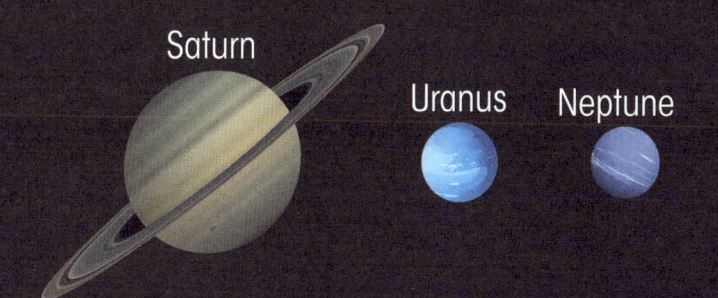

Saturn

Uranus

Neptune

Bonus
Could people really live on Mars?

We need to have water, shelter, food and air to survive.

How could we get those on Mars?

Water – There is some water on Mars, but it's underground and frozen into ice.

Shelter – People could live underground, or in special domes.

Bonus

How would people breathe and grow food?

Food – There is no soil on Mars to grow plants. But plants could be grown in huge water tanks. Huge domes could also work.

Air – A Mars rover is experimenting with making the poisonous gas on Mars into clean air.

Bonus

Green Mars on Red Alert!

When the biggest storm yet hit the Green Mars Inc domes on Mars, two hero school kids saved the day!

The Green Mars Inc base on Mars has just had a success with their first batch of Mars strawberries. But if it wasn't for two kids, years of work could have been lost.

Bo and Darian had a brave and ingenious idea to use their maglev hover boards to ride through some old cable tunnels on Mars. They managed to get some powerpacks out to the base just in the nick of time, before the plants died.

Now some of the scientists are learning to ride maglev boards so they can use these tunnels in emergencies.

Bo said: "It was scary at times but we looked after each other."

Darian said: "I'm not sure adults will be able to ride like we can, but I don't mind helping them!"

About the author

A bit about me …

Two years ago I made being an author my job, giving up teaching after 20 years, and it's a dream come true! I live right on the south coast of England with my husband, two sons, a dog and a cat. We all enjoy swimming in the sea…except the cat!

Lindsay Galvin

How did you get into writing?

I've always loved reading so I decided about 12 years ago I would try writing a book. I'd never written a story since school, but I loved it, so I kept learning and getting better at it until finally that book was published!

Is there anything in this book that relates to your own experiences?

I have a brother and a sister, so I understand that one minute you can be enemies, and the next minute the best of friends!

What do you hope readers will get out of the book?
I hope readers have a lot of fun imagining what it's like to zoom around on a hover board, and maybe write their own stories about something they'd love to try.

What is it like for you to write?
Sometimes fireworks go off in my brain, the characters come to life, and the real world disappears. Other times the words just don't come out right, and it's very difficult and tiring trying to get it right.

Would you like to go to Mars, if you could?
It would depend on how comfortable the ride was! I am adventurous, but only when I can get a good night's sleep …

Which of the characters do you most identify with?
Probably Bo and Darian's mum as I love science and plants, and I don't know if I'd be very good at hoverboarding!

Have you written a graphic novel before?
This is my first graphic novel and I enjoyed the challenge. In other novels, the words do all the talking, but in a graphic novel, the pictures tell the story too.

About the illustrator

What made you want to be an illustrator?

I've always liked to draw and loved comics and cartoons. Being an illustrator just seemed like a perfect job for me.

How did you get into illustration?

Alan Brown

I studied illustration at Uni, before working as a storyboard artist and graphic designer. I then picked up the courage to go freelance and haven't looked back, working with loads of great clients along the way.

What did you like best about illustrating this book?

I love skateboarding and sci-fi so it was all fun to draw.

What was the most difficult thing about illustrating this book?

Nothing really, it was a smooth job. I really enjoyed it.

Is there anything in this book that relates to your own experiences?

I used to skateboard until I broke my wrist which isn't ideal if you draw for a living... also I'm currently growing strawberries!

How do you bring characters to life in illustrations?

Hopefully, like in this book, the characters are 100 percent there in the script. All I had to do is draw them as I saw them ... and turn up the punk levels!

Would you like to go to Mars one day if you could?

Oh no ... I like trees and Mars is just orange rock.

Did you have to do any research to illustrate this book? What did you find out?

The only research I did was for the Mars terrain and the domes they lived in.

How is illustrating a graphic novel different from illustrating other kinds of children's book?

Comic book art has more space to tell the story. With a single page illustration, you have to tell the story with one image and try and squeeze everything in.

Book chat

Which character did you like best, and why?

Did your mood change while you were reading the book? If so, how?

If you could change one thing about this book, what would it be?

If you had to give the book a new title, what would you choose?

Which part of the book did you like best, and why?

Did this book remind you of anything you have experienced in real life?

Which scene stands out most for you? Why?

Do you think Darian changed between the start of the story and the end? If so, how?

Book challenge:

Design your own robot companion.

Published by Collins
An imprint of HarperCollins*Publishers*

The News Building
1 London Bridge Street
London SE1 9GF
UK

Macken House
39/40 Mayor Street Upper
Dublin 1
D01 C9W8
Ireland

Text © Lindsay Galvin 2023
Design and illustrations © HarperCollins*Publishers* Limited 2023

10 9 8 7 6

ISBN 978-0-00-862472-9

All rights reserved. No part of this publication may be reproduced, stored in a retrieval system, or transmitted in any form by any means, electronic, mechanical, photocopying, recording or otherwise, without the prior written permission of the Publisher or a licence permitting restricted copying in the United Kingdom issued by the Copyright Licensing Agency Ltd, 5th Floor, Shackleton House, 4 Battle Bridge Lane, London SE1 2HX.

British Library Cataloguing-in-Publication Data
A catalogue record for this publication is available from the British Library.

Download the teaching notes and word cards to accompany this book at:
http://littlewandle.org.uk/signupfluency/

Get the latest Collins Big Cat news at
collins.co.uk/collinsbigcat

Author: Lindsay Galvin
Illustrator: Alan Brown (Advocate Art)
Publisher: Lizzie Catford
Product manager and
   commissioning editor: Caroline Green
Series editor: Charlotte Raby
Development editor: Catherine Baker
Project manager: Emily Hooton
Content editor: Daniela Mora Chavarría
Copyeditor: Sally Byford
Phonics reviewer: Rachel Russ
Proofreader: Gaynor Spry
Cover designer: Sarah Finan
Typesetter: 2Hoots Publishing Services Ltd
Production controller: Katharine Willard

Collins would like to thank the teachers and children at the following schools who took part in the trialling of Big Cat for Little Wandle Fluency: Burley And Woodhead Church of England Primary School; Chesterton Primary School; Lady Margaret Primary School; Little Sutton Primary School; Parsloes Primary School.

Printed and bound in the UK

MIX
Paper | Supporting
responsible forestry
FSC™ C007454

This book contains FSC™ certified paper and other controlled sources to ensure responsible forest management.

For more information visit:
www.harpercollins.co.uk/green

Acknowledgements
The publishers gratefully acknowledge the permission granted to reproduce the copyright material in this book. Every effort has been made to trace copyright holders and to obtain their permission for the use of copyright material. The publishers will gladly receive any information enabling them to rectify any error or omission at the first opportunity.
p60 Lexus/Sipa/Shutterstock, p61 cyo bo/Shutterstock, pp64–65 Pavel Chagochkin/Shutterstock, p66 Claus Lunau/Science Photo Library, p67 Merlin74/Shutterstock.